PAPER CRAFTS
FOR
MARDI GRAS

Randel McGee

Enslow Elementary
an imprint of
Enslow Publishers, Inc.
40 Industrial Road
Box 398
Berkeley Heights, NJ 07922
USA

http://www.enslow.com

Dedicated to my cousin Michael McGee and his family, my friends Armondo &
Melissa Love, and Dianne de las Casas,
who know how to celebrate Mardi Gras in style!
Laissez Rouler les Bons Temps!

This book meets the National Standards for Arts Education.

Enslow Elementary, an imprint of Enslow Publishers, Inc.
Enslow Elementary® is a registered trademark of Enslow Publishers, Inc.

Copyright © 2012 by Randel McGee

All rights reserved.

No part of this book may be reproduced by any means
without the written permission of the publisher.

Library of Congress Cataloging-in-Publication Data

McGee, Randel.
    Paper crafts for Mardi Gras / Randel McGee.
        p. cm. — (Paper craft fun for holidays)
    Includes bibliographical references and index.
    Summary: "Explains the significance of Mardi Gras and how to make Mardi Gras themed crafts out of paper"—
        Provided by publisher.
    ISBN 978-0-7660-3724-3
    1. Carnival decorations—Louisiana—New Orleans—Juvenile literature. 2. Paper work—Louisiana—New Orleans—
        Juvenile literature. I. Title.
    TT900.C37M354 2012
    745.594'10976335—dc22   2010013616

Paperback ISBN: 978-1-59845-334-8

Printed in the United States of America

052011 Lake Book Manufacturing, Inc., Melrose Park, IL

10 9 8 7 6 5 4 3 2 1

To Our Readers: We have done our best to make sure all Internet Addresses in this book were active and appropriate when we went to press. However, the author and the publisher have no control over and assume no liability for the material available on those Internet sites or on other Web sites they may link to. Any comments or suggestions can be sent by e-mail to comments@enslow.com or to the address on the back cover.

Every effort has been made to locate all copyright holders of material used in this book. If any errors or omissions have occurred, corrections will be made in future editions of this book.

♻ Enslow Publishers, Inc., is committed to printing our books on recycled paper. The paper in every book contains 10% to 30% post-consumer waste (PCW). The cover board on the outside of each book contains 100% PCW. Our goal is to do our part to help young people and the environment too!

Illustration Credits: Crafts prepared by Randel McGee; photography by Nicole diMella/Enslow Publishers, Inc.

Cover Illustration: Crafts prepared by Randel McGee; photography by Nicole diMella/Enslow Publishers, Inc.

CONTENTS

AUTHOR'S NOTE: Many of the materials used in making these crafts may be found by using recycled paper products. The author uses such recycled items as cereal boxes and similar packaging for light cardboard, manila folders for card stock paper, leftover pieces of wrapping paper, and so forth. This not only reduces the cost of the projects but is also a great way to reuse and recycle paper. Be sure to ask an adult for permission before using any recycled paper products.

The projects in this book were created for this particular holiday. However, I invite readers to be imaginative and find new ways to use the ideas in this book to create different projects of their own. Please feel free to share pictures of your work with me through www.mcgeeproductions.com. Happy Crafting!

MARDI GRAS!

Let's plan a party! Everyone likes to wear masks and dress up, so we will make it a costume party. Let's have a special cake. Let's pass out party favors and prizes! Let's make it BIG, with marching bands and parades in the street! One day is not enough for all the fun, so let's plan on a whole week! How many should we invite? How about one million friends? Let's call it Mardi Gras!

Mardi Gras is French for "Fat Tuesday." This is the day before Ash Wednesday, the traditional beginning of Lent. Lent is a forty-day period of fasting and penitence observed by many Christian churches. Lent ends on Easter Sunday. Before beginning Lent, people will join together for parties and feasts. Mardi Gras has become a famous tradition in several cities, with New Orleans, Louisiana, and Mobile, Alabama, having two of the most well-known celebrations in North America.

In 1699, the French explorer Sieur d'Iberville (born Pierre Le Moyne) and his crew made camp not far from present-day New Orleans. They named the place Point du Mardi Gras in honor of the holiday and had their own celebration. As the population of the area grew, so did the

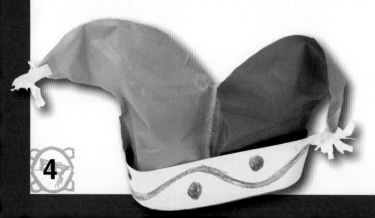

Mardi Gras celebrations. In the mid-1800s, many "krewes" (pronounced "crooz"), or clubs, were formed to plan parties, parades, and other special events to celebrate Mardi Gras. In 1872, the Krewe of Rex, the king of all the krewes, declared the official colors of Mardi Gras to be purple, green, and gold (representing justice, faith, and power).

In New Orleans today, there are many krewes that plan their own parades, colorful floats, fancy costumes, and grand balls to celebrate Mardi Gras. During the parades, thousands of people line the streets to see the floats, enjoy the music, and try to catch the special gifts and prizes that are thrown from the floats into the crowds. These gifts, called "throws," are usually beautiful beaded necklaces or shiny aluminum doubloons (coins) that people collect.

King cakes are a traditional treat during Mardi Gras. It is in memory of the three kings who searched for the baby Jesus. The cake has one nut or plastic baby baked inside to represent the baby Jesus. The person who finds the "baby" in his piece of cake will have good luck AND be responsible for bringing the cake the next year.

Other countries have similar celebrations on the same date. Many towns in France celebrate Mardi Gras. Many countries in Central and South America and the Caribbean have "Carnival." In Brazil it is called "Carnaval," and in Venice, Italy, they have "Carnivale." All these are celebrated with masks and costumes, music and parades. Let's make our own Mardi Gras party with the crafts that follow!

THE COLUMBINA MASK

The Columbina mask comes from the Carnivale celebrations of Venice, Italy. This half mask is decorated with swirling designs that look like flowers, butterflies, or fantasy creatures. It is colored gold and silver and decorated with ribbons. The mask is held in place with a handheld rod to make it easy to put on and take off.

WHAT YOU WILL NEED

- pencil
- tracing paper
- light cardboard or poster board, 8 x 4 inches
- scissors
- paintbrush
- white and glitter glue
- clear tape (optional)
- silver or gold wrapping paper or aluminum foil
- 12 x ¼-inch wooden dowel
- acrylic paint (optional)
- ribbon or crepe paper in different colors

WHAT TO DO

1. Use tracing paper and a pencil to transfer the black pattern lines from page 42 to the light cardboard or poster board and cut out the pattern.

2. Use a moist paintbrush to spread white glue over the front of the cardboard mask.

3. Place silver or gold wrapping paper (or aluminum foil) on the glued surface of the mask and smooth it out. Let dry.

4. Use scissors to trim the wrapping paper around the edge of the mask and the eye holes.

5. Use tracing paper to transfer the gray design lines of the pattern to the mask.

6. Decorate the mask with glitter glue on pattern lines or as you wish. Let dry.

7. Paint the dowel with
acrylic paint and let dry.

8. Glue or tape the dowel to the back and side
of the mask and decorate the dowel with ribbons or
crepe paper as you wish.

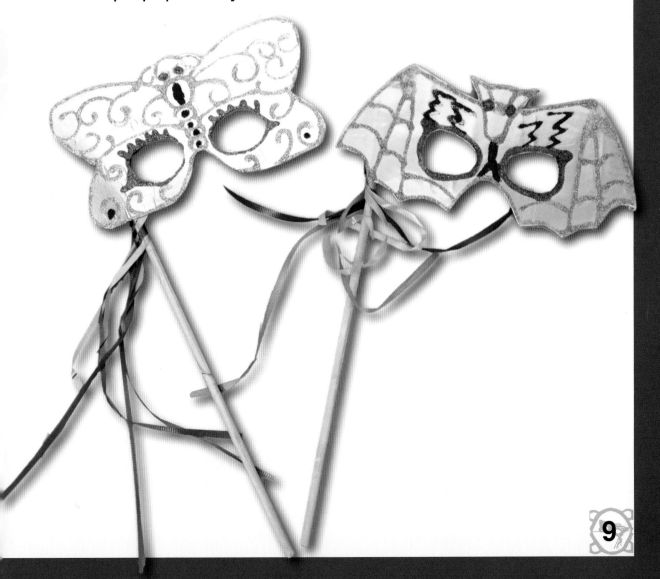

PAPER BEAD "THROW" NECKLACE

What a parade! The streets are lined with people of all ages! Huge, colorful floats are coming down the street. Costumed and masked people are perched all over the floats. As the crowds cheer, the costumed helpers throw glittering treasures to reward the parade watchers. Many of these "throws," as the treasures are called, are brightly colored necklaces worn by both girls and boys to show their Mardi Gras spirit. Show your Mardi Gras spirit with this paper bead necklace that you can make.

WHAT YOU WILL NEED

- ✎ wrapping paper in green, purple, and gold
- ✎ scissors
- ✎ thin yarn
- ✎ white glue
- ✎ drinking straws

WHAT TO DO

1. Cut strips from the wrapping paper that are 2 feet long and an inch wide on one end and ¼ inch wide on the other end.

2. Cut at least twenty-one of these paper bead strips.

3. Measure and cut 36 inches of yarn. Put a 1-inch line of glue on one end of the yarn. Let dry.

4. Put a thin line of glue along the length of the wrapping paper strip on the plain side. Fasten the wider end of the strip to the drinking straw. Carefully wind the strip on itself around the straw to form a thick bead. Repeat this until the straw has many paper beads on it. Let the beads dry on the straw.

5. Cut the drinking straw at the edges of the beads.

6. Tie a large knot in the end of the yarn that was not treated with glue. Thread the dried glue end of the yarn through the beads.

7. Tie the ends of the yarn together to form your necklace.

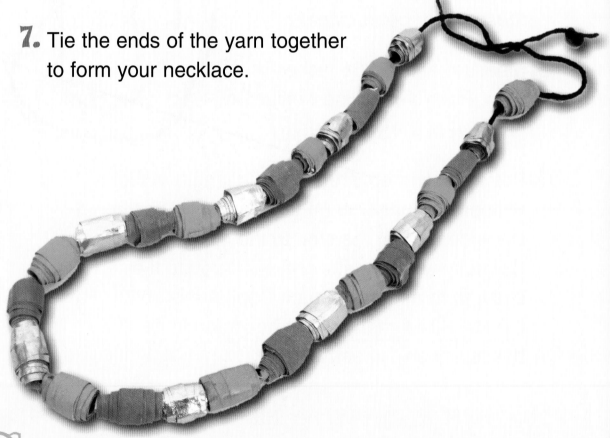

Mardi Gras Rhythm Maker

New Orleans, Louisiana, is famous for its jazz and rhythm and blues bands. Music is an important part of the Mardi Gras celebration. Marching bands are in every parade. Lively rhythms fill the air! You can get into the beat with your own Mardi Gras rhythm maker.

What you will need

- tracing paper
- pencil
- card stock
- scissors
- toilet tissue tube
- clear tape
- white glue
- small dry beans or unpopped popcorn
- construction paper in green, purple, and yellow
- crepe paper streamers (optional)
- ribbon (optional)

13

What to Do

1. Use the tracing paper and pencil to transfer the pattern from page 36 to the card stock. Cut out the pattern from the card stock.

2. Bend down the flaps on the card stock pattern. Use tape or glue to fasten the flaps of one pattern piece to one end of the toilet tissue tube.

3. Put about a teaspoon of beans or unpopped popcorn in the tube.

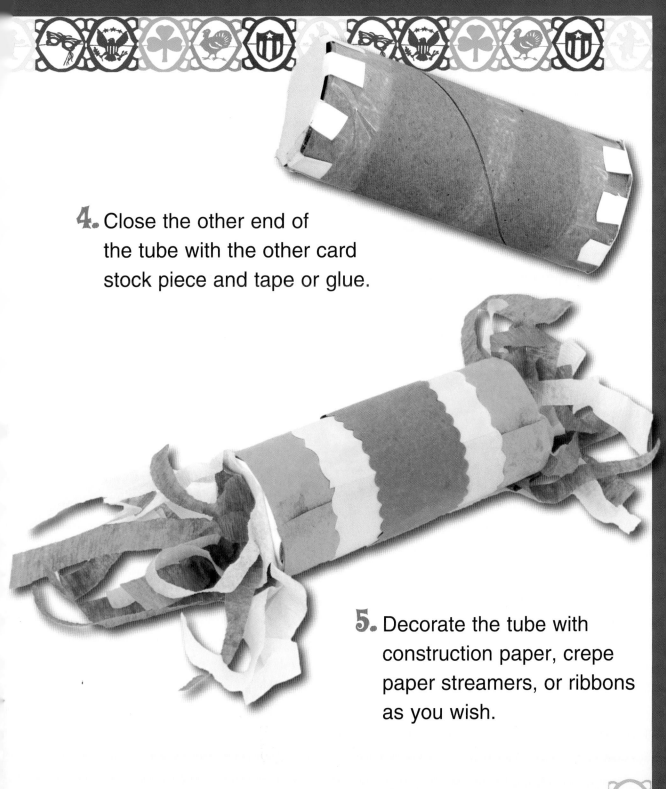

4. Close the other end of the tube with the other card stock piece and tape or glue.

5. Decorate the tube with construction paper, crepe paper streamers, or ribbons as you wish.

15

Gold Doubloon Necklace

A doubloon is a Spanish gold coin that was used in America until the 1800s. Shiny aluminum doubloons are used in Mardi Gras jewelry and as gifts thrown from the floats. Make your own treasure by following the directions below!

What you will need

- tracing paper
- pencil
- light cardboard
- scissors
- white glue
- gold wrapping paper
- gold glitter glue
- drinking straws (to make paper beads) (optional)
- hole punch
- thin yarn

WHAT TO DO

1. Use the tracing paper and pencil to transfer the doubloon pattern from page 36 to the light cardboard. Cut out at least nine doubloons.

2. Cover one side of the doubloons with a light coating of white glue and place them on the plain side of the wrapping paper. Let dry. Do the same on the other side of the doubloons, so that both sides are covered with gold wrapping paper. Let dry.

3. Cut out each doubloon from the wrapping paper.

4. Decorate one side of the doubloon with gold glitter glue as you wish. Let dry.

5. Wrap a drinking straw with a bit of gold wrapping paper and glue it in place. Let dry.

6. Cut the decorated drinking straws into one-inch pieces.

7. Use the hole punch to punch holes in the gold doubloons as suggested in the pattern.

8. Thread the yarn through the straw pieces and through the holes in the doubloons in an alternating pattern. Tie the ends of the yarn together to form a necklace.

Full Face Mask

Since the beginning of time, people have worn masks to portray other characters or creatures and live for a moment in fantasy. Masks and costumes have always been an important part of Mardi Gras. The masks can be of any animal or person, real or imaginary. Most Mardi Gras masks are of smiling human faces with elaborate decorations or clown designs. Use your imagination with this basic mask pattern to create your own Mardi Gras character or creature.

What you will need

- white card stock— 8 ½ x 11 inches
- tracing paper
- pencil
- scissors
- construction paper in any color
- glue or tape
- markers or crayons
- craft feathers (optional)
- masking tape
- yarn—2 pieces about 12 inches long

WHAT TO DO

1. Fold the white card stock in half lengthwise.

2. Use the tracing paper and pencil to transfer the pattern from page 37 to the folded card stock.

3. Cut out the pattern and unfold it.

21

4. Decorate the mask using markers, crayons, construction paper, and feathers as you wish.

5. Overlap the two flaps at the center of the top and bottom and glue or tape them together.

6. Use masking tape to tape a 12-inch piece of yarn to each side of the back of the mask. Make sure that the yarn is long enough to tie around your head.

7. Have an adult help you tie the mask around your head.

JESTER'S CAP

Once upon a time, kings and queens usually had a jester to make them laugh! The jester wore a colorful suit and a hat with two floppy points, like donkey ears. The jester is a popular character in Mardi Gras parades and balls.

WHAT YOU WILL NEED

- poster board
- scissors
- tracing paper
- pencil
- 2 plastic table covers—different colors *
- glue stick
- markers and crayons
- plastic jewels (optional)
- glitter glue (optional)
- clear tape
- yarn (optional)
- crepe paper streamers (optional)

*AUTHOR'S NOTE: Plastic table covers are lightweight, are inexpensive, and come in a wide variety of colors. They can be found at many department and craft stores in the party section.

WHAT TO DO

1. Cut the poster board to make a strip 2 x 24 inches.

2. Use tracing paper and a pencil to transfer the pattern from page 43 to the table covers. Make two copies of Color 1 and two copies of Color 2. Cut out the patterns.

3. Lay a pattern of each color in front of you. Use the glue stick along the edge of Line B on Color 1 and fasten it to the edge of Line B on Color 2. Do the same with the other pattern pieces. Let dry.

4. Use the glue stick around the outside edge of the pattern, and then place one pattern on top of the other so that they match up evenly. Do not put any glue on Line A. Let dry.

5. Decorate one side of the poster board strip with markers, crayons, plastic jewels, or glitter glue as you wish.

6. Have an adult help you bend the poster board strip into a circle that will comfortably fit your head. Use tape to fasten the ends together.

7. Use tape to fasten Line A of your pattern piece around the inside of the poster board ring.

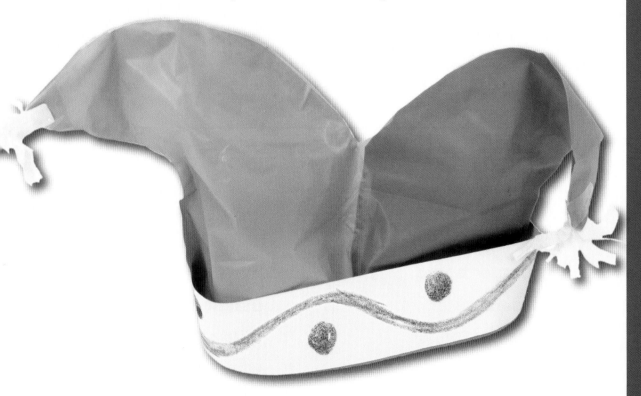

8. Use tape and bits of yarn or crepe paper streamers to decorate the tips of your jester's cap.

ROYALTY CROWN

Every Mardi Gras social club has a king and queen to rule over its parade and party each year. The king and queen have a royal court of dukes and duchesses and knights and ladies-in-waiting like the royal courts of old Europe. The king and queen wear crowns and very decorative royal clothes. You can become a king or queen for Mardi Gras with this crown that you can make.

WHAT YOU WILL NEED

- poster board
- scissors
- tracing paper
- pencil
- markers and crayons
- plastic jewels

- glitter glue
- plastic table cover
- glue stick
- white glue
- clear tape

WHAT TO DO

1. Cut a strip of poster board
   4 x 13 inches. Fold it in
   half so that the short ends meet.

2. Use the tracing paper and a pencil to
   transfer the pattern from page 38 to the folded poster
   board strip. Be sure to place the dotted line of the
   pattern on the fold of the strip.

3. Cut along the solid black lines of the pattern.

4. Open the strip and decorate it with markers, crayons, plastic jewels, and glitter glue as you wish. Let dry.

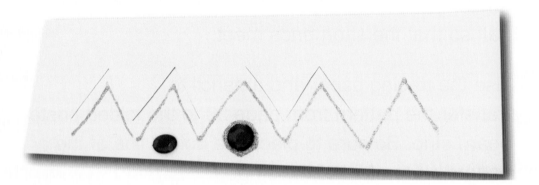

5. Use the tracing paper and a pencil to transfer the pattern from page 39 to the plastic table cover. Cut two pieces of the pattern.

6. Use a glue stick to glue the edges of the plastic table cover pattern together. Do not glue along line A. Let dry.

7. Fold the poster board pattern along the dotted fold lines on the ends. Use a drop of white glue to glue the ends together. Let dry.

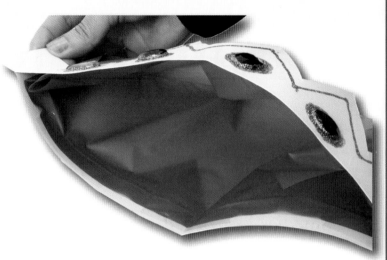

8. Open the crown enough to tape Line A of the plastic piece around the inside of the crown. Open the crown gently and place it on your head.

Moving Mardi Gras Mask Card

The Harlequin clown is a popular character in traditional comedies from France and Italy. It is also popular in Mardi Gras parades and decorations. Harlequin clowns can be either male or female. They are recognized by their white and black makeup, colorful costumes with diamond patterns, and jester's caps. They do acrobatics and make funny faces to entertain the Mardi Gras crowds. This moving Mardi Gras mask looks like a Harlequin. Give it as a greeting card or use it as a decoration to entertain your friends.

What You Will Need

- ✎ tracing paper
- ✎ pencil
- ✎ card stock—2 sheets
- ✎ markers or crayons
- ✎ scissors
- ✎ paper fastener
- ✎ white glue
- ✎ construction paper

WHAT TO DO

1. Use the tracing paper and pencil to transfer patterns 1 and 2 from pages 40 and 41 to the sheets of card stock.

2. Color and decorate both patterns. One page will be the main picture, and the other will be the moving parts.

3. Cut along the solid black lines of both the pattern pages.

4. Carefully slip the jester's cap through the slit at the top of the Harlequin's face, and slip the tongue through the slit at the mouth. The tab should stick out slightly from the side.

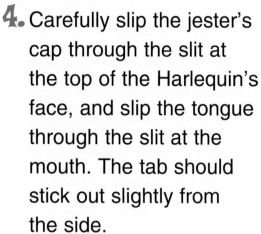

5. Push a paper fastener through the picture at the *X* and through the moving part behind it. Secure the paper fastener in place.

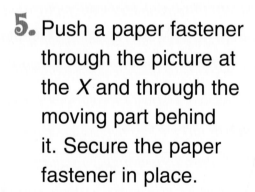

6. Glue the nose to the paper fastener. Let dry.

7. Glue the top and bottom back edges of the picture to a piece of construction paper. Let dry.

8. Write a Mardi Gras greeting if you wish. Make the face move by gently moving the tab up and down.

PATTERNS

The percentages included on the patterns tell you how much to enlarge or shrink the image using a copier. Most copiers and printers have an adjustable size/percentage feature to change the size of an image when you print it. After you print the patterns to their true sizes, cut them out or use tracing paper to copy them. Ask an adult to help you trace and cut the shapes.

Mardi Gras Rhythm Maker

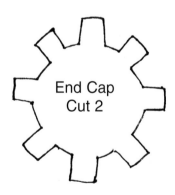

End Cap
Cut 2

At 100%

Gold Doubloon Necklace

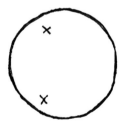

At 100%

Full Face Mask Pattern

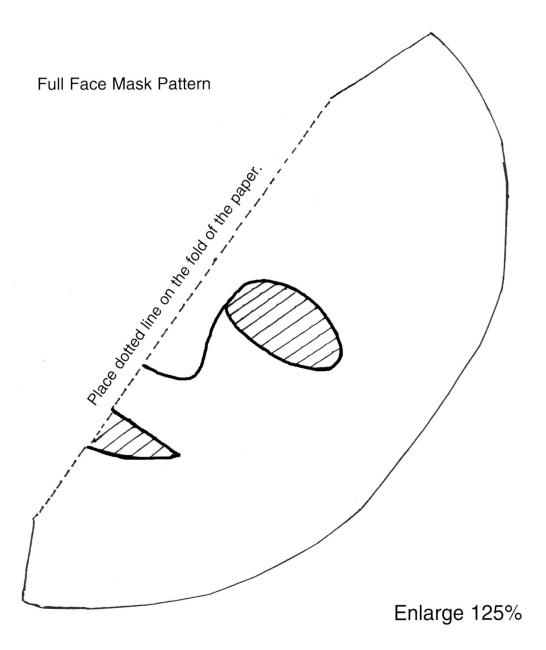

Place dotted line on the fold of the paper.

Enlarge 125%

Royalty Crown

Crown Pattern

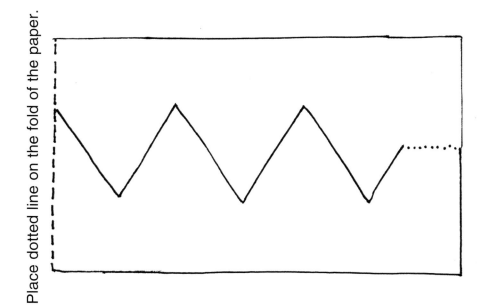

Place dotted line on the fold of the paper.

Enlarge 200%

Royalty Crown

Inside Cap Pattern

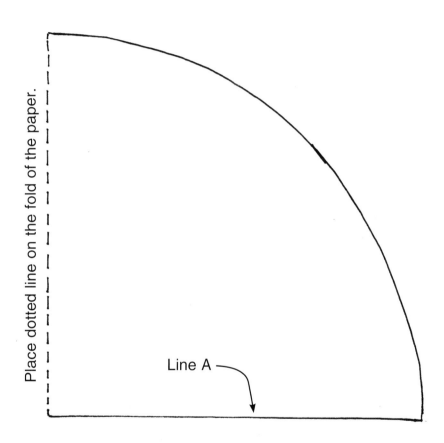

Place dotted line on the fold of the paper.

Line A

Enlarge 200%

Moving Mardi Gras Mask Card
Main Pattern

At 100%

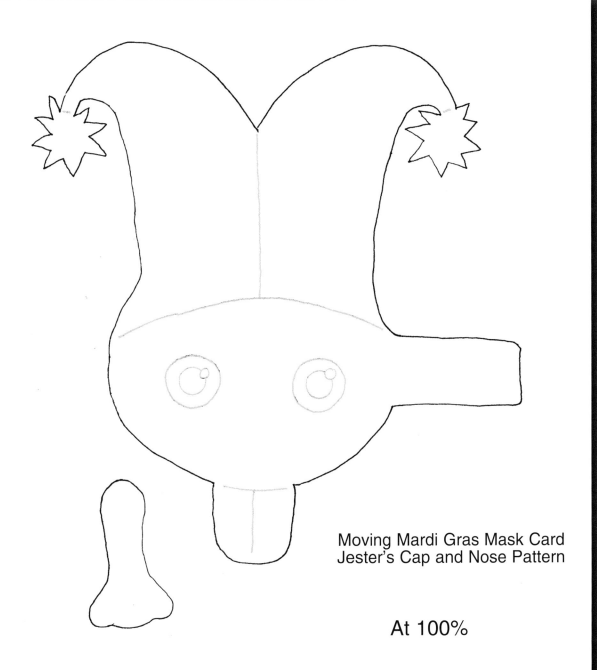

Moving Mardi Gras Mask Card
Jester's Cap and Nose Pattern

At 100%

Columbina Mask
Butterfly Pattern

Enlarge 125%

Columbina Mask
Dragon Pattern

Enlarge 125%

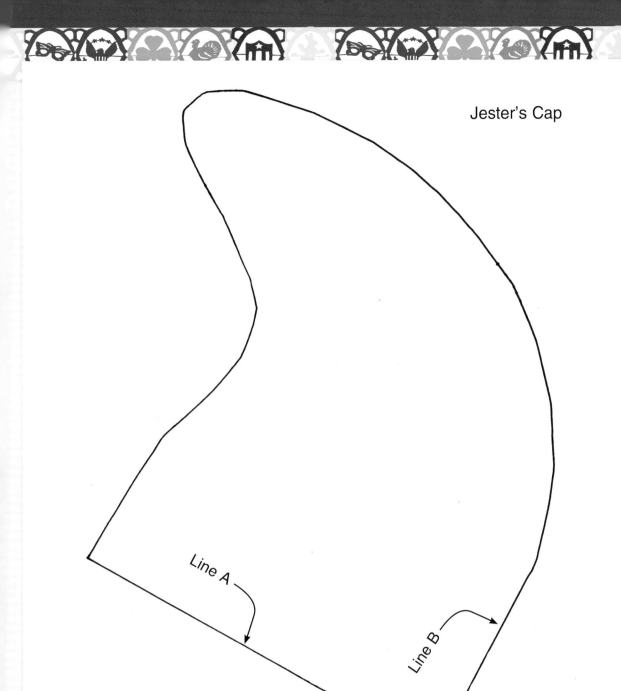

Jester's Cap

Line A

Line B

Enlarge 125%

READ ABOUT

Books

Aloian, Molly. *Mardi Gras and Carnival.* New York: Crabtree, 2010.

Berg, Elizabeth. *Festivals of the World: The United States.* Tarrytown, N.Y.: Marshall Cavendish Benchmark, 2011.

Heinrichs, Ann. *Mardi Gras.* Chanhassen, Minn.: Child's World, 2006.

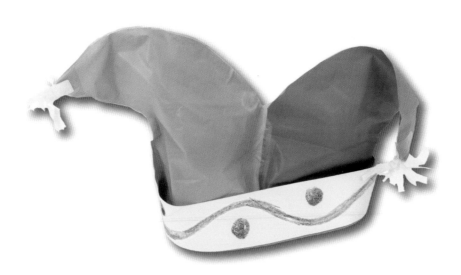

Internet Addresses

DLTK's: Mardi Gras Activities

<http://www.dltk-kids.com/crafts/mardigras/index.htm>

Activity Village: Mardi Gras for Kids

<http://www.activityvillage.co.uk/mardi_gras.htm>

KinderArt: Mardi Gras Crafts

<http://www.kinderart.com/
  seasons/mardigras.shtml>

Visit Randel McGee's Web site at
<http://www.mcgeeproductions.com>

INDEX

A

acrobatics, 32
Alabama, 4
America, 16

B

ball (celebration), 5, 24
beads, 10
blues (music), 13
Brazil, 5

C

cake, 4, 5
Carnaval (Brazil), 5
Carnival, 5
Carnivale (Italy), 5, 6
Christian (church), 4
clown, 32
club, 5, 28
Columbina Mask, 6
costume, 4, 5, 20

D

decoration, 20, 32
doubloons, 5, 16

E

Easter, 4
Europe, 28

F

Fat Tuesday, 4
float, 5, 10, 16
France, 5, 32
Full Face Mask, 20

G

Gold Doubloon Necklace, 16

H

half mask, 6
Harlequin, 32

I

Italy, 5, 6, 32

J

jazz, 13
jester, 24, 25
Jester's Cap, 24, 32
Jesus, 5

K

king, 5, 24, 28
king cake, 5
krewes, 5

L

Lent, 4
Louisiana, 4, 13

M

Mardi Gras, 4, 5, 10, 13, 20, 24, 28, 32
Mardi Gras Rhythm Maker, 13
mask, 4, 20
Mobile (Alabama), 4
Moving Mardi Gras Mask Card, 32
music, 5, 13

N

necklace, 5, 10, 16
New Orleans, 4, 5, 13
North America, 4

P

Paper Bead "Throw" Necklace, 10
parade, 4, 5, 10, 24, 28, 32
party, 4, 28
Point du Mardi Gras, 4

Q

queen, 24, 28

R

Rex (Krewe of), 5
royal court, 28
Royalty Crown, 28

S

Sieur D'Iberville, 4
South America, 5
Spanish, 16

T

three kings, 5
throws (gifts), 5, 10
treasures, 10, 16

V

Venice (Italy), 5, 6

ABOUT THE AUTHOR

Randel McGee has been playing with paper and scissors for as long as he can remember. As soon as he was able to get a library card, he would go to the library and find the books that showed paper crafts, check them out, take them home, and try almost every craft in the book. He still checks out books on paper crafts at the library, but he also buys books to add to his own library and researches paper-craft sites on the Internet.

McGee says, "I begin by making copies of simple crafts or designs I see in books. Once I get the idea of how something is made, I begin to make changes to make the designs more personal. After a lot of trial and error, I find ways to do something new and different that is all my own. That's when the fun begins!"

McGee has also liked singing and acting from a young age. He graduated from college with a degree in children's theater and specialized in puppetry. After college, he taught himself ventriloquism and started performing at libraries and schools with a friendly dragon puppet named Groark. "Randel McGee and Groark" have toured throughout the

United States and Asia, sharing their fun shows with young and old alike. Groark is the star of two award-winning video series for elementary school students on character education: *Getting Along With Groark* and *The Six Pillars of Character.*

In the 1990s, McGee combined his love of making things with paper with

his love of telling stories. He tells stories while making pictures cut from paper to illustrate the tales he tells. The famous author Hans Christian Andersen also made cut-paper pictures when he told stories. McGee portrays Andersen in storytelling performances around the world.

Besides performing and making things, McGee, with the help of his wife, Marsha, likes showing librarians, teachers, fellow artists, and children the fun and educational experiences they can have with paper crafts, storytelling, drama, and puppetry. Randel McGee has belonged to the Guild of American Papercutters, the National Storytelling Network, and the International Ventriloquists' Association. He has been a regional director for the Puppeteers of America, Inc., and past president of UNIMA-USA, an international puppetry organization. He has been active in working with children and scouts in his community and church for many years. He and his wife live in California. They are the parents of five grown children who are all talented artists and performers.